The Gift of Death

What the Final Teacher Shows Us About Life

Dean Nelson

Table of Contents

Author's Note

Thank you for reading The Gift of Death. It was written with deep reverence for life and with a willingness to look openly at its end.

I chose to write this book without religious framing, not to dismiss anyone's faith but to offer an alternative; one grounded in reflection, compassion, and intellectual honesty. My intention is not to convert but to connect, not to instruct but to invite.

I write as a philosopher, a secular humanist—someone who finds meaning and ethics through human reason and compassion rather than religious doctrine—and as a fellow traveler who has wrestled with the mystery of death. Over time, I have come to see death not only as an end but also as a mirror; one that reflects what we truly value, what we have postponed, and what we fear to face.

This book emerged from a recognition that death, perhaps our most universal experience, has become our most avoided conversation. I do not write as someone who has conquered the fear of dying, but as someone still learning to live honestly with that fear. My hope is that by sharing this walk through mortality's landscape, we might all find our footing a little more surely, and our appreciation for life a little deeper.

This book is not a treatise, nor a solution; it is a walk. It began with a quiet idea—to speak honestly and gently about death without dogma or denial, not to solve the mystery but to sit beside it for a while. I wanted to create a space where we could think and feel our way toward acceptance, where the unknown could be faced not with resistance but with curiosity.

Each chapter is a reflection, an invitation, a pause. They are meant to be read slowly, to be revisited, or even skipped depending on where your heart rests in the moment. There is no single path through this terrain; death, like life, is deeply personal.

The book is organized into twelve brief chapters, each one exploring an aspect of death's gift—its ability to clarify, to awaken, and to teach us how to live more fully. They are designed to serve both as solitary meditations and as shared readings, especially for those who are nearing death or accompanying someone who is. These chapters are not lessons in grief or philosophy, but simple offerings for contemplation.

If this book leaves you with questions, memories, or new conversations, I welcome that. The intention was never to end the dialogue but to spark it—to open a space where thought, feeling, and presence can coexist. You are invited to continue this conversation with yourself, with those you love, or with me.

Writing The Gift of Death has reminded me that facing mortality is not about surrendering to despair but about deepening our commitment to life. Death humbles us, yes, but it also refines our gratitude. It shows us what matters most when everything else falls away. In walking toward it, we walk closer to truth, to love, and to one another.

Thank you for walking a little further into the
quiet with me.

The Gift of Death

Prologue: Death, the Quiet Teacher

We speak of many things. We plan our lives, set goals, and share our joys and struggles. But we rarely speak of death, not directly, not honestly, and not without a whisper of fear or discomfort.

In this culture of achievement and denial, death has become our final taboo. We hide it behind hospital curtains, euphemisms, and barely understood rituals. We try to outrun it with youth serums, cosmetic surgery, and wishful beliefs. We treat it as an enemy, a failure, a glitch in an otherwise endless stream of life.

But death is not a glitch, it is the frame.

This book is not about morbidity. It is about clarity. It is about what death can teach us, not when it comes for us but while we are still here to listen. For death is a teacher unlike any other; it strips away the unessential, it asks us to see what truly matters, it shows us what is real.

I do not write this book from a place of doctrine or dogma. There are no sacred texts here, no appeals to gods, heavens, or karmic ladders. I write as a human being who has wrestled with mortality, who has seen others go before me, and who has wondered, as you may have, what, if anything, lies on the other side.

More importantly, what should we do now, knowing we won't live forever?

This book is not a book of answers. It is a book of awakenings. If you are willing to look closely at death, you may find that it does not diminish life;

it sharpens it. It reveals its texture, urgency, and beauty. It reminds us that we do not have infinite chances to be kind, to create, to speak, and to love.

To confront death is not to dwell in sorrow but to rediscover purpose. It brings our scattered attention back to what matters most. It clarifies relationships. It gives weight to our words and depth to our actions. And it reminds us, often with painful honesty, that time is not something we own but something we borrow.

In cultures worldwide, wise traditions have taught people to "keep death in mind," not as a burden but as a lens. The Stoics wrote of memento mori, "remember you will die," not to depress but to ignite presence and purpose. The Buddhists reflected on impermanence, the understanding that clinging causes suffering and acceptance brings peace. In Christianity, death points to the promise of renewal and the importance of love, grace, and forgiveness. In Judaism, remembrance and ethical living are vital ways of honoring those who have passed. In Islam, death is seen as a return to the Creator, urging humility and responsibility in this life. Hinduism views death as a transition, part of the soul's journey toward liberation. Even secular traditions, rooted in science and humanism, invite us to reflect on our finitude, not to despair but to live more vividly.

Let us speak, at last, about death, not to rehearse despair but to discover meaning. We should not fear the end, but embrace the moment we are in.

Let death become our teacher, not a shadow. Let it show us how to live.

That is the gift it offers, if we are willing to unwrap it.

Chapter 1: What Is Death?

We speak of death as if we understand it. We've all heard the words: "passed away," "gone to a better place," "no longer with us." But behind the euphemisms lies a mystery we rarely confront directly; what is death? Not just biologically, but experientially, philosophically, and personally?

At its most basic level, death is the cessation of biological function. The heart stops. The lungs deflate. The brain goes quiet. And yet, defining the exact moment when life ends is more complicated than it sounds.

In the past, death was determined by the absence of breath or heartbeat. But with modern medicine, these signs are no longer definitive.

Today, death is often defined by the irreversible loss of brain activity, what we call brain death. Even that definition can be murky. What if parts of the brain are still flickering? What about consciousness?

Consciousness, the experience of being, is central to our sense of life. It is what makes us feel alive. But where does it go when we die? Is it extinguished like a candle blown out, or does it dissolve gradually like mist dissipating into sunlight? Science has not yet provided a definitive answer, though many hypotheses abound. Some argue that consciousness is an emergent property of the brain, a result of complex neural activity. Others propose that consciousness may be a more fundamental feature of reality, like gravity or time.

One thing is clear: when the brain is irreparably damaged, consciousness as we know it disappears. Identity fades. Memory collapses. The presumed self, that fragile constellation of thoughts, feelings, and history, dissolves into silence.

But beyond the clinical definitions lies something more unsettling: the recognition that this biological event, this cessation, this silence, awaits each of us. It is one thing to understand death medically, it is another to feel it personally. To move from "what is death?" to "what will my death be?"

Death, then, is not just a biological event, it is a personal vanishing.

This is why death unnerves us so profoundly. It is not only that we cease to be, it is that everything we know, everything we are, seems to vanish with us.

I've thought about death for as long as I can remember, not abstractly but personally. My father died by suicide when I was young. It wasn't just grief that settled into our home, it was silence. That silence became my introduction to mortality, not through answers but through absence. Even now, decades later, it shapes how I walk beside the idea of death.

My walks in nature are more pleasurable. My interactions with strangers are more engaging. My time spent with friends is more meaningful. My family relations are deeper, far more important, and thoroughly satisfying.

The Gift of Death

For much of our lives, we live as if death does not apply to us. We keep it hidden, out of sight and out of mind. We tend to avoid it conversationally. But death is not avoidable. Without it, meaning would collapse.

The fear of death, though deeply personal, is also cultural. We inherit it through stories, traditions, and the unspoken rules of society. From childhood, some of us are shielded from the reality of death. We're told not to think about it or given imaginative narratives to contain the discomfort. We are conditioned, subtly and persistently, to treat death as a catastrophe instead of a fact.

Some people fear death because of religious conditioning, threats of punishment, unknown judgment, or endless separation. Others fear the absence of anything, the void. But what if we leaned into it instead of trying to overcome this fear? What if fear were a signpost, not of danger but of depth?

Let's consider several quotes, some known and some unknown, from those at or near their death. They provide various perspectives on how people perceive death when it is near.

"Death is not the opposite of life, but a part of it." — Haruki Murakami

"Some people are so afraid to die that they never begin to live." — Unknown

"To live in hearts we leave behind is not to die." — Thomas Campbell

Similar reflections surface in end-of-life care and are not unusual. They remind us that the real problem with death is not just that it comes, it is that it forces us to question whether we've truly lived.

So let us ask again: what is death?

It is a mirror. It is a threshold. It is a teacher.

And perhaps, more than anything, it is the silent companion that shapes every moment we call life.

Pause for Reflection

Some believe this life is merely the prelude to something greater, a brief test before eternity begins. But what if it is not? What if this is the whole story, the only chapter we are given? Would you read it more slowly, more carefully? Would you write it differently?

Chapter 2: The Awakening

There comes a moment, quiet and unremarkable, often in the space between sleeping and waking, when the truth lands differently. Not as concept but as certainty. Not "people die," but "I will die." The shift is subtle but seismic. Everything looks the same, but the light has changed. You are still you, yet you are also temporary. And once that truth settles in, it never quite leaves.

It does not arrive with trumpets. There is no thunderclap, no announcement. The realization that you are going to die comes quietly, often in an unguarded moment; a nighttime thought, a sentence overheard, a cold wind that suddenly feels too cold. It is no longer abstract. It is you, not a concept but an inescapable truth. And when that truth lands, your life begins to change, often in small and hidden ways.

Some spend their entire lives keeping death at a distance, trying not to look it in the eye. But whether we turn toward it or away from it, death does not lose patience; it simply waits.

This realization that your story has an end is not a punishment. It is not a flaw in the design. It is, paradoxically, what gives the narrative of your life its beauty, its clarity, its context. Without the certainty of an ending, we might never feel compelled to begin.

Philosopher Shelly Kagan, a renowned Yale professor who has spent decades studying death and meaning, put it this way: "It's because life is short that it matters what we do. If we had forever, we could afford to drift. But we don't."

Mortality sharpens the moment. It slices through our illusions and distractions. It makes ordinary days extraordinary. When you know the clock is ticking, you learn to listen more closely, love more deeply, and waste less time on things that do not nourish you profoundly.

Pause for Reflection

When did you first truly understand—not intellectually but viscerally—that you would someday die? How did that realization change the way you moved through your days?

There is a strange freedom that comes with accepting death, not as a threat but as a companion; not malevolent, just genuine. Death walks with us. It does not need to make a scene to shape our behavior. Its presence, once acknowledged, quietly rearranges our priorities.

What we pursue changes, what we forgive changes, and above all, what we value begins to shift.

We are not wired to grasp our mortality all at once. It is too vast, too final. Instead, the truth seeps in slowly, like early morning fog rolling in off a lake. At first, it feels theoretical, like learning that the sun will eventually burn out or that entire galaxies are drifting apart. But then, one day, it is not just death—it is your death. Suddenly, the timeline snaps into focus. It is no longer an idea. It is a deadline.

The Gift of Death

It is not meant to frighten. Fear is one response, but not the only one. Some feel relief; a strange kind of clarity, a sharp-edged honesty that demands a different way of living.

We begin to audit our days.

What am I doing with my time?
Why am I pretending this matters when it doesn't?
Why am I spending so much energy avoiding discomfort, silence, or the truth?

When death feels distant, we live as if we have infinite chances to try again, to call back, to apologize, to show up differently. But mortality is the ultimate deadline. It does not negotiate extensions. This awareness does not demand panic; it invites prioritization. When you truly grasp that your time is finite, you begin to audit not just your schedule, but your soul.

In a deathless life, we could indulge in every distraction. But in this one, we are called, not always gently, to focus. Mortality does not just take; it refines. It distills us. We start asking questions we might rather avoid. Sometimes, we find meaning. Other times, we find only questions. Yet even that is a kind of progress.

Some people become kinder once they understand their time is finite. Others become braver. A few become quieter, more attuned to the small rhythms of daily life; the opening of a new book to read, the sound of birds singing in the garden, the emergence of a smile on the face of a stranger.

It is not morbid to befriend death. It is foolish not to. It is a teacher no one invites, but everyone must face. And what it teaches, if you are willing to listen, is not how to die—but how to live.

Pause for Reflection

If you truly knew that your time here was limited, how would you speak to the people you love? What would you stop pretending not to feel? And if you believe in something beyond this life, does that deepen or dilute your sense of urgency here and now?

Once we stop keeping death at a safe distance, we find that it was never far at all. We begin to notice its shape in every goodbye, its breath behind every birthday candle. Some days it whispers. Other days it roars. And still, we live.

But awakening to death does not mean we immediately accept it. Often, the first response is resistance, not logical but emotional. Why should I die? Why should anyone? We rail against the unfairness, even when no promise was ever made.

Then comes grief, not always for a specific person but for time—lost time, misused time, the time we now realize we will never get back. That grief is quiet and difficult to name, but it shapes us. It is the ache of missed opportunities and the echo of paths not taken.

Some try to reconcile death through diets, disciplines, rituals, and beliefs. Others deny it altogether, refusing to speak the word, avoiding hospitals and funerals, treating youth as eternal. But denial does not erase what waits. It only delays our peace with it.

Eventually, if we are honest, we begin to listen—not to death itself, for it has no voice—but to what its presence reveals about us; our priorities, our fears, our attachments, and our capacity to care. Death, when faced directly, becomes a mirror. What we see in it depends on how willing we are to look.

This first realization—"I am going to die"—is not the end of the story. It is the beginning of a new kind of awareness that grows sharper with time. It may not give us answers, but it changes the questions we ask. And sometimes, that is enough.

Pause for Reflection

Many religions treat death as the beginning of something greater. But what if death is simply the end—final, irreversible, and natural? Would that diminish the value of life or multiply it? What if impermanence is not a flaw in the system but the very thing that makes meaning possible?

Chapter 3: What We Do With the Truth

If we cannot escape death, many of us try to outwit it, not by avoiding it but by leaving something behind. We write books. We carve our names into stone. We build businesses, raise children, and plant trees. While often beautiful, these acts are sometimes laced with quiet desperation: Remember me. Prove I was here.

Legacy becomes the modern afterlife.

But legacy is not immortality. Memories fade. Statues crumble. Even the most significant works eventually vanish or are forgotten. And yet, we do it anyway. Why?

Because these gestures are not only about the future; they are about now. They are how we cope with the weight of vanishing, how we translate fear into art and anxiety into action. Whether or not they endure, these acts help us live with clarity in the face of the unknown.

Pause for Reflection

If you could be remembered for one thing, what would it be? And if you knew no one would remember you, would your actions still carry meaning?

Culture gives us many tools for responding to death. Religion offers one path, through ritual, story, and structure. Philosophy offers another, through inquiry, contemplation, and practice. Both can be powerful. However, both can be misused. Religion can promise false certainty, and philosophy can avoid emotion through abstraction.

And then there are those who try not to respond at all. They turn away, distract themselves, and numb out. Often, this avoidance is not even conscious. It becomes a kind of background hum—unspoken, automatic. They stay busy. They chase goals. They pour energy into things that keep the mind occupied. Some of the busiest people you will ever meet are running from a thought they do not realize they are avoiding.

But avoidance is costly. What we do not face directly tends to leak out sideways, as anxiety, resentment, or the hollow ache of a life only half-lived.

Paradoxically, death can be a stabilizer. When acknowledged, it clarifies, distills, and helps us shed the roles we were performing so we can return to something closer to truth.

It is not about being fearless. It is about being honest.

Death has always inspired ritual. We light candles, write names, and gather in silence or song. These gestures are often framed within religion, but their deeper purpose runs older and wider than any tradition. Ritual is how we mark significance. It is how we say: This matters. This person mattered. I am trying to carry what cannot be carried.

Even in secular lives, rituals form. We scatter ashes in lakes or forests. We reread old letters. We plant trees in memory. We walk the same trail each year on the birthday of someone no longer here. These are not just sentimental habits; they are acts of meaning-making. They anchor grief. They create continuity where death has broken the line.

You do not need belief in an afterlife to grieve with depth. And you do not need dogma to say goodbye with reverence. What you need is presence, honesty, and a willingness to feel what comes.

Pause for Reflection

Is there a ritual you have created or witnessed that helped mark a loss? What made it meaningful? Was it the form or the feeling behind it?

The Gift of Death

And yet, for many, it is not ritual that changes them. It is rupture.

When someone you love dies, especially when it is unexpected or early, the world shifts—not just emotionally but perceptually. The colors dull. Time bends. The old assumptions no longer hold. We begin living in a different register, one where nothing feels guaranteed.

In this disoriented space, people often undergo a kind of second awakening. The first was intellectual: I will die someday. The second is visceral: Death is here. It has already touched me. It can happen again.

Some become more anxious. Others become more open. Many become both.

The Gift of Death

A close loss does not just make death real—it makes life fragile. And once that fragility is seen, it is hard to unsee. That is not always a bad thing. It can make us gentler, more grateful, and less willing to waste time. It can also make us pause before we speak, listen longer, and love better.

Most of us live somewhere between extremes. We neither entirely deny death nor fully embrace it. Instead, we weave around it. Some days, we forget it altogether. Other days, it shows up uninvited, in a diagnosis, a phone call, or a memory. We might not fear death constantly, but it lingers at the edge of the frame, waiting for quiet moments to reappear.

This tension is not weakness. It is human. It reflects the complexity of being conscious creatures who can imagine our own disappearance. Even when we accept death in principle, we may resist it in practice. We meditate in the morning, then curse the traffic jam by afternoon. We talk about impermanence, then obsess over losing our youth. There is no clear line between fear and acceptance. Most days, we carry both.

You can welcome death as a teacher and still dread its arrival. You can believe in letting go and still grasp tightly to those you love. There is no contradiction in this. There is only life, lived honestly.

Pause for Reflection

Is there a part of you that accepts death and another part that resists it? What would it feel like to let both exist without forcing one to win?

The Gift of Death

This in-between space, this flickering between fear and acceptance, is often where the real work happens. It is where meaning is built, not assumed, where courage becomes practice, not posture, and where we learn to live with open eyes, even if they sometimes fill with tears.

And maybe that is the best we can hope for: not total fearlessness, not perfect peace, but presence. A willingness to face what is, to speak honestly about it, and to live more fully because of it.

We do not need to conquer death to befriend it. We do not need to silence our fear to live honestly beside it. It is enough to stop pretending. We need to look at what is inevitable and still choose to build, to love, to speak gently, and to mean what we say.

The Gift of Death

Death does not make life meaningless. It makes it vivid, a bit more urgent, finite in the way that all beauty is finite.

So, we continue our quiet rituals, unfinished conversations, and paradoxes. We laugh and make plans, knowing they might be broken. We cry and reach for each other anyway. We tell stories. We tell the truth. We make meaning not because we must, but because we can.

If we are lucky, or simply awake, we begin to live not in fear of the end but with a new intimacy with the present.

Pause for Reflection

What if the goal is not to overcome death but to live in its presence with integrity, curiosity, and care?

Chapter 4: The Fear of Ceasing

Why We Resist the End

Most people don't fear death because they understand it. They fear it because they don't, and because they can't. Death is the one certainty we carry, yet it remains the one thing we're least prepared for. This is psychological, cultural, and deeply, stubbornly human.

To fear death is not just to fear pain or finality. It is to fear annihilation, not of the body, but of the self; the vanishing of memory, identity, and story. The world goes on, yet we do not. And that, for many, is a terror more profound than any mythic punishment.

We also fear what we can't imagine. The brain, built to anticipate outcomes, has no framework for nonexistence. It is like asking the eye to see its own blindness. We try to picture what it's like to be dead, but we can't. We are still there in the imagination. Consciousness cannot conceive of its own absence.

That dissonance doesn't just confuse us, it unsettles us. And often, it frightens us. Not because death is always painful; many deaths are not. It frightens us because it remains unknowable. And what we cannot know, we often come to fear.

Culturally, fear can be magnified by silence. In many modern societies, death has been sanitized, outsourced, and euphemized. We no longer die at home, as in centuries past, but behind machines, curtains, and closed doors. Our language reflects our discomfort: people "pass," "transition," and "go to sleep." These phrases may obscure the finality of death and, in doing so, deepen the mystery. Most people use these terms out of respect for those dying and those surrounding them, which is understandable. Yet, if we were raised to speak openly of death as a final departure and not a temporary exit from life, the pain might not be quite so unbearable.

For many, religion steps into that gap, offering stories of reunion, reward, or continuation. And yet, even the faithful often harbor private doubts. For those without belief, death may feel like a wall with nothing behind it; a full stop, a blank.

The fear of death, when faced directly, can bring focus. It reminds us that our time is limited and, therefore, valuable. That truth, uncomfortable as it is, can stir gratitude. It can spark reflection. It can propel change.

"Seasons don't fear the reaper, nor do the wind, the sun, or the rain. We can be like they are."
— Blue Öyster Cult, Don't Fear the Reaper

As we age, the shape of our fear evolves. Young people may also fear dying; the sudden, the unfair. But older people often fear not having lived. Regret becomes louder than death itself. This, too, is part of the human condition. We don't just want to live; we want our lives to mean something. We want to leave a trace, a ripple, a memory that proves we were here.

To resist death is not irrational. It is written into our biology. Evolution favors survival. But when we refuse to even look at death, when we push it into the margins, we give it unnecessary power. We begin to live as if our lives are infinite, and in doing so, we waste the very thing we are trying to protect.

The challenge is not to erase the fear of death, but to understand it; to name it, to learn its edges, and to sit with it long enough for it to stop being a monster under the bed and become a part of the room we already occupy.

Pause for Reflection

When fear of death arises, what is it pointing to? Is it a fear of pain, of disappearance, or of leaving something unfinished?

Only then can the fear begin to shift, not into comfort necessarily, but into perspective, priority, and a deeper courage; not the courage to live forever, but the courage to live fully before we do not.

When we are young, death feels fictional. It belongs to other people far away; grandparents, strangers, names in obituaries. Even when someone young dies, we see it as an exception, a mistake in the system.

Something in us refuses to believe that death applies to us.

This isn't arrogance; it is insulation. Youth is a kind of existential bubble, not because we think we are invincible, but because the concept of not being has not yet taken root. The body is strong.

The future feels limitless. Time stretches out like a blank highway with no visible exit.

In that state of mind, it is easy to delay. It is easy to defer the things that matter most; forgiveness, honesty, risk, depth. The illusion of immortality feeds the fantasy that there will always be more time. Later becomes the catch-all. Later is when we will apologize. Later is when we will start writing, or stop pretending, or finally tell someone we love them.

But "later" is a mirage. It always seems near, until it isn't.

Pause for Reflection

What have you told yourself can wait? And if tomorrow did not come, would it still be the right choice?

The Gift of Death

It often takes a loss, a brush with mortality, a friend's diagnosis, or a parent's death to crack the shell. Suddenly, the illusion vanishes. Time reveals its sharp edge. The story turns.

This breaking is painful, but it can also be sacred. It can mark the beginning of a different kind of life, not necessarily more dramatic, but more awake.

Even after the illusion of immortality fades, many of us still do not confront death directly. We move faster. We get busier. We accumulate more; more experiences, more opinions, more obligations. But beneath the momentum, something softer often lingers: fear.

We may not say it aloud. We may not even know it is there. But we feel it in the quiet moments; the unease when we stop moving, the discomfort of silence, the need to scroll, check, and do. These aren't always signs of laziness or distraction. Sometimes, they are symptoms of unacknowledged mortality. We run because we are afraid to stand still.

Regret rarely shows up all at once. It accrues. The conversation we avoided. The person we pushed away. The art we never made. The truths we swallowed. We think we are protecting ourselves by waiting, but often, we are only postponing the pain of not living in alignment with who we are.

And so, when death does come close, through diagnosis, age, or loss, what hurts most is not the prospect of dying, but the realization that we have been living as if we would not.

The Gift of Death

Pause for Reflection

If your life ended unexpectedly, what would you wish you had done, or said, while there was still time?

This isn't about perfection. No one escapes life without some unfinished pages. But there is a difference between a life ending suddenly and a life never really inhabited.

The fear of ceasing often whispers: Did I matter? Did I love well? Did I show up? These questions need honest answers. And when we begin living from that place, not of fear but of clarity, the fear starts to change.

It does not disappear, but it becomes quieter; less like a warning siren and more like a tuning fork gently asking us to realign with what matters.

The Gift of Death

Not everyone transforms their fear of death into dread or denial. For some, it becomes a kind of reverence, not for death itself, but for life seen through death's lens. They begin to live with more intention. They speak more slowly. Listen more closely. They no longer move through the day as if it is a rehearsal.

There is something sacred in that shift. What once felt like a threat, you will end, now becomes a guide: this matters. A walk becomes an event. A conversation becomes a memory. A breath becomes enough.

Reverence does not mean solemnity. It means attentiveness, gratitude; a kind of moral clarity that comes not from fear of punishment but from awareness of impermanence.

Some people begin to choose differently. They leave jobs that make them feel invisible. They reach out to the estranged. They forgive, not because the past changes but because the future shrinks. They stop postponing joy.

Pause for Reflection

What would a life of quiet reverence look like for you, not someday, but now? What would you stop waiting for?

This is not about erasing fear. It is about letting it teach, letting it point to what matters, letting it break through our defenses long enough to help us come home, not to safety but to truth.

We do not need to banish the fear of death. We need to learn from it; to let it show us what is unfinished, to let it sharpen our attention, and, maybe, to let it soften our hearts.

When we do, we shift from resisting death to honoring life. And in that shift, the fear becomes quieter; not gone, just less prominent.

Living with the fear of death is not a deficiency. It is part of being human. But when that fear is buried, ignored, or disguised, it tends to rule us from the shadows. When it is named, gently and clearly, it begins to change shape.

Fear becomes inquiry. Inquiry becomes clarity. Clarity becomes action.

And with time, we begin to walk alongside the fear instead of trying to outrun it. We stop bargaining with immortality and begin living in the time we actually have.

We may still grieve our impermanence and long for more. But we also begin to see the gift hidden inside the fear; a deeper commitment to the life we have, to live not forever but fully, with honesty, courage, and compassion until we do not.

Understanding our fear is the first step. The second is recognizing how our culture shapes that fear, often in ways we don't even notice.

Pause for Reflection

What would it mean to walk beside the fear of death instead of away from it?

Chapter 5: Cultural Masks

How We Hide Death in Plain Sight

Fear of death is deeply personal, but it is also profoundly cultural. The stories we inherit about dying—what it means, how it should happen, and whether we should speak of it at all—shape our ability to face it honestly. Before we can truly befriend our mortality, we must first examine the masks our culture places over death's face.

In many parts of the modern world, death is often concealed in subtle yet powerful ways, and the families of those dying may not be as involved as in centuries past. We move the dying into facilities. We soften our words. We cushion the impact with distractions and a thousand well-intentioned avoidance strategies.

The Gift of Death

In this case, we do not face death; we stage-manage it.

And in doing so, we lose something essential, not just about death, but about life itself.

In past generations, death was often close. It happened in the home, within reach of the family. Children saw grandparents grow frail, heard the final breaths, and witnessed grief not as a private breakdown but as a communal ritual. Death played a visible and natural role in the story of life. It was not an interruption but a completion.

Today, in many cultures, that intimacy has eroded. Death is delayed by machines, hidden behind curtains, and described with softened language. Although the intentions are good, the end result often lacks the personal involvement and emotional connection the dying person might need most.

Pause for Reflection

What euphemisms for death did you grow up hearing? How might your relationship with mortality be different if you had been raised to speak of death as naturally as birth?

Nowhere is the cultural masking of death more apparent than in modern medicine. We have made extraordinary advancements, and they have saved countless lives. But alongside this progress, a quieter shift has occurred; the transition of death from a human event to a medical failure.

We have created a strange paradox; we are extraordinarily skilled at postponing death, yet remarkably unprepared for dying. Hospitals save lives daily, and we are grateful. But in the process, we have also medicalized death itself, turning it from a human passage into a medical procedure. The question becomes not "How can we help this person die well?" but "What can we do to prevent this person from dying at all?"

Doctors are trained to fix, to fight, and to extend life, often with deep compassion and purpose. In this context, dying becomes something to prevent rather than something to engage with. The body turns into a battleground. The patient becomes a case to manage. The deathbed, too often, becomes a terminal procedure rather than a sacred moment of peace or reflection.

This is no one person's fault. It is systemic. In many hospitals, a "good death" is delayed, not dignified. The focus remains on interventions; another treatment, another tube, another hour. Rarely is the question asked: at what cost, and for whom? Dying may be seen as a problem to solve, not a process to accompany.

Pause for Reflection

Have you ever witnessed someone die "under care," yet far from comfort? What was gained, and what might have been lost?

This is not an argument against medicine. Those in the medical field are true heroes, and I am deeply grateful for their tireless efforts to sustain and extend life. This is an argument for balance— for restoring death to its rightful place within both palliative care and the collective imagination. We must once again make room for the human experience of dying; emotional, relational, and spiritual, not merely biological.

We must allow for the possibility that a life well lived might include a death well met.

Medicine can sometimes sterilize death, but the media often trivializes it.

In television and film, death is frequent but weightless. Characters die violently, instantly, dramatically; then the camera cuts away, the music swells, and life moves on. There is little lingering. No post-mortem silence. No aftermath of sorting through clothes, voicemail messages, or unpaid bills.

We consume thousands of deaths in fiction, but rarely see one fully lived.

The Gift of Death

In news media, death is often summarized in numbers—casualties, statistics, body counts. This gives us a sense of scale and urgency, but it also distances us. Many journalists work to counter this by sharing the names, faces, and stories behind the numbers. They remind us that every life lost is not just a statistic but a world interrupted.

This saturation without intimacy leaves a mark. We grow desensitized, or perhaps disoriented. Some people have seen thousands of fictional deaths but have never sat beside someone dying. They know the sound cue of a gunshot but not the sound of a final breath. They have cried at a scripted funeral but have no idea what to say at a real one.

The Gift of Death

Pause for Reflection

How has the media shaped your expectations of what death looks like? Does it match what you have experienced?

The result is a strange paradox. We are surrounded by images of death yet unprepared for its reality. We see it everywhere and nowhere. It is performed but rarely honored.

When death finally arrives, many feel betrayed by how different it looks. It is not clean or dramatic. It is slow, tender, messy, and often silent. There is no orchestral score, no profound final words, only breath and skin and waiting and love.

To truly understand death, to face it without flinching, we must unlearn what much of our media has taught us. We must stop confusing representation with reverence.

Grief, like death, has also been privatized. In many modern cultures, there is no roadmap, no communal rite, and no real allowance for grief's unpredictable shape. There may be a brief acknowledgment, a few days off, a condolence card, and then the unspoken message arrives: move on.

We do not grieve in public. We manage it in private. Preferably quickly, preferably quietly.

This emotional isolation leaves many feeling abandoned. They are not only mourning a person but also mourning in a world that seems unwilling to engage with their loss.

Some try to speak, but they sense discomfort in the room. Conversations grow awkward. Invitations fade. Eyes look away. So the mourner learns to perform normalcy—to smile through the ache, to say "I'm fine" when they are anything but.

Pause for Reflection

Have you ever hidden your grief to make others more comfortable? What did that cost you?

Grief is not a failure of coping. It is an expression of love. It is the continuation of connection in the absence of presence. Yet we often treat it as a weakness, something to "get over" rather than something to live with.

The Gift of Death

This cultural resistance to grief is another mask, another way of denying death, even after it has happened. But grief, like death, does not vanish simply because we ignore it. It lingers. It reshapes. It becomes part of the person who carries it— quieter, perhaps, but never gone.

When we begin to remove these cultural masks— the clichés, the performances, the staged narratives—we start to see death not as a catastrophe but as a truth. Not something to avoid, but something to meet.

And when we meet it, honestly and unmasked, we recover something we did not realize we had lost; the dignity of being fully human, all the way to the end. Once we look past the illusions and evasions, we can begin to ask the more honest questions about the time we actually have.

Pause for Reflection

What would it look like to speak more openly about death in your family, your friendships, and your own heart?

In the chapters ahead, we turn from how death is hidden to how we use the time that remains. Death may take the body, but it cannot touch the meaning we create while we are here.

Chapter 6: The Time We're Given

Death does not just end our time; it reshapes how we experience it. The moment we truly grasp our mortality, time changes. It feels faster and sharper, sometimes more urgent and sometimes more sacred. The casualness with which we once spoke of "later" begins to dissolve.

When we are young, or when death feels distant, time is elastic. We postpone dreams. We tell ourselves we will call them next week, take the trip next year, and say what we really mean when the time feels right. But death puts pressure on the myth of "later." It pulls the curtain back on our assumptions about how much time we truly have.

It is not just that life is short; it is that we do not know how short.

That awareness is not a threat; it is a lens, a way of seeing. When you carry the awareness of death, even quietly, you become more deliberate. You begin to notice how often time is wasted not in rest but in avoidance, procrastination, resentment, and distraction. Not stillness, but drift.

Pause for Reflection

If you knew that you would be gone a year from now, what would you stop putting off? What would become irrelevant overnight?

Awareness of time's limits can make life feel more urgent, but it can also make it feel more expansive. A single conversation can feel deeper.

The Gift of Death

A simple afternoon, more radiant. Presence intensifies. You begin to feel the weight of each hour, not as a burden but as a privilege.

This does not mean rushing. In fact, the most profound awareness of death often leads to slowing down. You stop sprinting toward some imagined milestone and start listening to what your life is asking of you now.

Some people describe this shift as becoming more awake. Others say it feels as though life finally became real.

Time becomes more than a resource. It becomes a mirror, quietly reflecting how closely we are living in alignment with our values. When death feels far away, it is easy to delay hard conversations, postpone acts of kindness, or remain in situations that numb rather than nourish. But when the horizon draws closer, through age, illness, or loss, time begins to ask difficult questions.

What am I doing with the time I have?
Who am I spending it on?
Does how I spend my days reflect what I claim to believe?

These are not abstract questions. They carry a moral weight. Time, in this sense, becomes a kind of truth serum. You cannot hide behind ambition, excuses, or performance for long. How we spend our time becomes how we tell the truth about our lives.

This shift often brings clarity. Things once deemed important begin to fade—status, approval, accumulation. In their place, other values surface: kindness, curiosity, stillness, and love. Many people, when faced with the reality of their limited time, do not want more achievement. They want more authenticity, presence, honesty, and less pretending in their relationships.

Pause for Reflection

What if your calendar, your actual use of time, was the most honest autobiography you ever wrote? What would it say about what you value?

This awareness does not mean that every moment must be monumental. We are not machines of efficiency. But it does mean that time becomes sacred in a new way—not because it is always productive, but because it is always disappearing.

In this light, saying "no" becomes easier. So does saying "yes." You begin to prioritize not only what feels good but what feels right. You stop trying to be everything to everyone. You start choosing based not on fear or obligation but on alignment with something truer—your authentic self, not your performing self.

One of the quiet gifts of living in death's shadow is this: the pressure to prove, possess, and perform begins to loosen. Slowly and subtly, you start to wonder whether you have been chasing things that never truly mattered to you.

The awareness of death does not always ignite ambition; sometimes, it extinguishes it. Not out of despair, but clarity. You realize that more is not always better, that success, as commonly defined, may not align with joy. You do not need to read every book, visit every country, or fulfill every expectation placed upon you to live a beautiful life.

Mortality becomes an invitation to simplify, to strip away the noise, to step off the treadmill of "not enough" and ask: What is already here? What do I already have that I have been too busy to appreciate?

In that shift, something unexpected can emerge— peace. Not the kind marketed by gurus or purchased on retreats, but a quieter peace, the kind that arrives when you stop needing everything to be extraordinary and instead learn to sit fully in the ordinary.

The sound of someone's voice you love. The song of a mockingbird. The laughter of a friend.

These become sacred, not because they are rare but because they are perishable.

Pause for Reflection

What would it mean to stop striving for more and honor what is already enough in your life? What might that free you from?

Letting go of the fantasy of "more" is not about giving up; it is about coming home—home to yourself, home to what matters, home to this life as it is, not as promised or imagined.

Some people fear this kind of acceptance. They confuse it with resignation. But simplicity is not surrender. It is a deep form of strength. It says: I know I do not need everything. I only need what is real.

The Gift of Death

Once viewed through the lens of mortality, time becomes more than a schedule to manage. It becomes a teacher, not loud or urgent, but persistent. It asks not how much we have done, but how fully we have been present while doing it. It asks not what we have earned, but what we have loved. Not how long we have lived, but how deeply we have shown up for the life unfolding right now.

And in answering those questions, something softens. The chasing slows. The judgment quiets. We begin to live not for legacy or applause, but for resonance—the kind that lives in small moments, kind gestures, and honest words.

Death does not demand greatness; it demands presence. And sometimes, presence is the greatest thing we can offer.

So we stop waiting for the perfect moment. We stop hoping to be ready. We say the thing. We hold the hand. We listen carefully. We begin to treat time not as something we manage, but as something we belong to.

Pause for Reflection

When your time comes, as it must, will you be able to say you showed up—not perfectly, not always, but with as much honesty, attention, and love as possible?

And maybe that is what death is offering us all along—not terror, not despair, but a deeper entry into life, one breath at a time.

Chapter 7: Living with Regret

Regret is the ghost of choices unmade. It lives in the quiet spaces between what was and what might have been. For many, the approach of death sharpens these ghosts, not because they arrive suddenly, but because they have always been there, waiting for our attention.

When death draws near, time shifts. What once felt infinite becomes finite. We review our lives with new clarity—and often, with ache. Words left unsaid. Paths not taken. Apologies unoffered. Kindnesses withheld. What we regret is not failure, but the moments where we were not fully ourselves.

Bronnie Ware, an Australian palliative care nurse, famously documented the top regrets of the dying. The most common? "I wish I'd had the courage to live a life true to myself, not the life others expected of me."

It is a powerful indictment, not of others, but of how we abandon our own voice.

Pause for Reflection

In what ways have you stayed silent, small, or safe to meet others' expectations? What would courage look like now?

Regret, however, is not the enemy. It is a form of awareness, the mind finally catching up to the heart. We regret because we care. We regret because we see more clearly now what mattered.

The Gift of Death

There is time, even late in life, to reconcile. To speak what has not been spoken. To make amends, even if symbolically. To write the letter. To say the name. To offer the forgiveness we once withheld—including to ourselves.

Self-forgiveness is often the hardest kind. We revisit our younger selves with adult eyes, forgetting how little we knew. We expect wisdom before we earn it. But regret can become compassion when we remember this: we did not know then what we know now. And even if we did, we may not have had the strength to act on it.

Some people carry regret like armor, using it to keep others, and themselves, at a distance. But we can learn to hold it differently: not as punishment, but as guidance. Regret can show us where we went dormant and where we can still wake up.

Pause for Reflection

Is there something you still blame yourself for? What would change if you viewed it as a signal for healing, not a sentence for guilt?

Not all regrets can be resolved. Sometimes, the person is gone. Sometimes, the opportunity has passed. In these cases, we can still honor what was unfinished. We can speak aloud what we wish we had said. We can light a candle. Write a letter we will never send. We can live differently now, in their memory or our own. Regret that cannot be undone can still be redeemed—by who we become because of it.

Living with regret does not mean being defined by it. It means making peace with imperfection. It means understanding that all lives are partial, unfinished, human. No one gets it all right. No one avoids every hurt. But we can choose, again and again, to live from what we have learned.

Pause for Reflection

What would it mean to carry your regret not as a weight, but as a teacher?

And when we do that, regret transforms. It stops chasing us and starts guiding us. It becomes not the shadow of what we did not do, but the light that shapes what we do next.

We cannot alter the past, but we can change how we live with it.

Interlude: Reflections of Dean

While writing this book, I found myself reflecting deeply on my past, and with that reflection came regret. The contemplative nature of this work stirred something within me. It was as if the scenes of my life were playing out before me again, not for judgment, but for understanding.

I saw moments when I had been dishonest with myself and with others. I failed to listen, to engage, or to show up. I saw how I had been selfish with my time, held onto grudges, and lacked the courage to stand up for what mattered—for myself and for others.

I saw the times I doubted myself, questioned my worth, and felt ashamed of who I had become. I remembered how I was not always fully present with my family, especially during my daughters' youth. I was consumed by a need to fix what I believed was broken in me. I carried heavy guilt over my father's suicide, convinced that healing myself would make me a better father. But healing, I now see, came at the cost of precious time I could never get back.

The healing I sought was real and necessary. But I wish I had understood then what I know now: presence does not require perfection. My daughters did not need me to be fixed; they needed me to be there. Fully, imperfectly, humanly there. The irony is that in trying to become a better father by healing myself, I missed countless opportunities to simply be their father.

I have too many regrets to list.

But with time and grace, I began to forgive myself, not all at once, but slowly, steadily. I changed, not into some perfected image, but into someone better.

Through the long, quiet conversations with myself, I came to understand the deeper meaning behind the words we wrote together. Every book I have written has changed me, even though it was drawn from my own thoughts and voice. There is something about seeing your words on the page that makes them more real, more powerful. They stop being ideas and become invitations.

What I have come to believe is this: it is never too late to change. It is never too late to be kind, to listen fully, and to let go of impatience, intolerance, or pride.

Even if I had only weeks to live, there would still be time to forgive. Time to make the call I have put off. Time to sit with someone and be fully present. Time to become the person I have always hoped to be.

Chapter 8: What Survives Us

Legacy, Memory, and the Echo of Influence?

Regret teaches us what we valued too late. But from that teaching comes possibility: the chance to live differently, to choose more consciously, to become the kind of person whose legacy is not perfection but presence. What we leave behind is not a record of our achievements but an echo of our love.

Legacy is often thought of as something grand, a name in a book, a building with a plaque, a line of descendants carrying forward our blood. But most of what truly survives us is quieter, more ordinary, and more powerful.

The Gift of Death

We leave traces in people, in how they remember our voice, our presence, our love. Our influence on others is often invisible while we are alive but deeply felt once we are gone, in the way we listened, the way we laughed, the way we made someone feel seen. These are the echoes that outlast us.

Psychiatrist Irvin Yalom called this rippling—the idea that each of us sets off waves in the lives of others—waves that continue moving outward, even when we are no longer here to watch. This is legacy in its most human form.

Pause for Reflection

What invisible ripples do you think you have left in the lives of others? And who is still rippling in yours?

Legacy also lives in stories. How someone talks about us at a kitchen table long after we are gone. The way our sayings or habits become family shorthand. These are not grand monuments, but they endure, and often they guide.

Of course, not all legacies are gentle. Some people leave behind wounds, burdens, or silence. And those, too, shape lives. But even there, influence can become transformoments, which I call moments of transformation. We are not just what we inherit. We are what we choose to carry and what we choose to lay down.

There are also legacies we never get to see. A kind word spoken to a stranger. A piece of wisdom passed casually but remembered. A generous act that changed someone's course without us ever knowing. These anonymous legacies may be the purest, given freely, with no need for recognition.

Pause for Reflection

Have you ever been changed by someone who did not know the impact they had? Might you have done the same for someone else?

Legacy is not a record. It is a resonance. It is what remains when the name fades. And the truth is, we do not get to choose precisely what survives. We only choose how we live and how much of ourselves we give to others along the way.

Some people are remembered for their great works. Others are remembered for how they made people feel. Some are not remembered by name at all, but their kindness becomes someone else's kindness. Their steadiness becomes someone else's strength. Their story becomes part of someone else's way of surviving. That, too, is legacy.

We may never know the full reach of our lives, but we can live in a way that allows those who follow us to feel something real, something human, something good, something true. That is what survives. That is what makes life—and death—meaningful.

Interlude: Walking Through Grief—A Guide for the Journey

Grief is not a problem to be solved but a territory to be navigated. It has its own geography, valleys of despair, plateaus of numbness, and unexpected peaks of memory that take your breath away. Unlike other life transitions, grief comes without clear directions. Yet there are landmarks most grievers recognize.

The Early Days

In the immediate aftermath of loss, your only job is to breathe. Everything else can wait. Grief in its rawest form demands nothing except that you continue existing. Maintain basic rhythms, eat small amounts regularly, accept help with logistics, honor your need for solitude or company. Create simple rituals: light a candle, look at photos, sit in their favorite chair. Small acts of remembrance provide comfort without overwhelming your depleted system.

The Waves

Grief arrives in waves, sometimes gentle swells and sometimes tsunamis. You might be fine for days, then suddenly sob in a grocery store. This is not regression; it is the natural rhythm of processing loss. Grief bursts are temporary. Triggers are everywhere—a song, a scent, someone's laugh. Physical symptoms are real: exhaustion, aches, brain fog. Create a "grief toolkit," including trusted contacts, comfort objects, and peaceful places to retreat.

The Middle Passage

Months into grief, you are caught between two realities: the one where they existed and the one where they do not. This liminal space is disorienting but necessary. You are learning to carry love in the absence of presence. Write letters to continue conversations. Keep some belongings, release others when ready. Honor significant dates intentionally. Seek professional support when family and friends feel insufficient; this is not failure but wisdom.

The Mythology of "Moving On"

Our culture treats grief as temporary, something to "get over." This is harmful. You do not move on from love; you learn to move forward with it. The goal is not to stop missing them but to carry their influence meaningfully. You can maintain a relationship with someone who has died through memory, values, and ongoing conversation. You can build a new life while honoring what was lost. Growth alongside grief is possible.

When to Seek Help

Professional support may be needed if you experience persistent inability to function after several months, substance use as primary coping, thoughts of self-harm, complete social withdrawal, inability to accept the reality of death, or intense guilt interfering with relationships.

The Ongoing Journey

Grief is not a phase you exit but a companion you learn to walk with. Years later, you may still have moments of acute missing. This is not failure; it is love. You do not recover from grief; you grow around it. In that growth, you discover that love is stronger than death, not because it prevents loss, but because it survives it.

Pause for Reflection

*Where are you in your grief journey? What support do you
need that you have not yet asked for?*

Chapter 9: The Lives We Touch

What We Leave Behind in Others

We all leave something behind. Whether or not we believe in an afterlife, we ripple forward, in gestures, in memories, in the quiet architecture of someone else's life. A word remembered, a kindness repeated, a piece of advice that lives on long after the voice that gave it has gone silent.

It is not about grandeur. It is about influence. We shape others through our presence, and they, in turn, carry part of us with them. This is not poetic optimism. It is observable truth. The way you held your child's hand. The way you listened to your friend. The time you said, "I believe in you," and meant it. These things matter. They echo.

Pause for Reflection

Who has shaped you, not through fame or greatness, but through presence? And what part of you might ripple forward into others?

We often think of legacy in monumental terms: buildings, books, achievements. But most of what we leave behind is smaller and quieter: how we made people feel, whether we helped them feel safe, and whether we showed up when it counted.

In this light, death does not erase us. It returns us to the people we touched, the stories we helped shape, and the lives we gently altered just by being ourselves.

Grief, in its strange way, is a form of continuation. We grieve because someone mattered, because they changed us. And even in their absence, they are still shaping our inner landscape, the way we think, the way we love, the way we pause at certain words because they used to say them too.

Grief wears different faces depending on how death arrives. Sudden loss—accident, heart attack, unexpected news—leaves us gasping, unfinished, reaching for words we will never get to say. Anticipated loss—illness, age, the slow goodbye—gives us time to prepare, but also to watch helplessly as someone we love fades by degrees. Neither is easier. Both require us to love in the presence of loss, to hold on while learning to let go.

When we grieve, we carry not just sorrow but memory, not just absence but influence. We begin

to trace their presence in our daily lives: the meals
we cook, the songs we cannot hear without
crying, the soft, intimate conversations shared
with a glass of wine by the campfire.

Sometimes, we live differently because of them.
We become gentler, more deliberate, more
generous. We stop taking things for granted. We
make different choices. And that, too, is legacy.

In this way, death does not sever connection. It
transforms it.

Pause for Reflection

*Whose presence do you still carry, not just in memory, but
in who you have become?*

Grief is not simply pain. It is a form of active remembrance. It says: You mattered. You still do. I am still becoming because of you. It can be overwhelming, yes, but it is also deeply human, a form of loyalty, a form of love.

Often, those we grieve continue to guide us. Not because we imagine them watching over us, but because they have become part of the moral and emotional compass we use to live. What would they have done? What would they say? Would they be proud of who I am becoming?

These are not just wistful questions. They are reminders that we do not live alone. No one ever really does.

When someone you care about is grieving, your instinct may be to fix, to comfort, to make it better. But grief is not a problem to solve; it is a love that has nowhere to go. Sometimes the most healing thing you can offer is not words but presence, not answers but acknowledgment. "I see how much they meant to you." "I cannot imagine your pain, but I am here." "Tell me about them." Simple phrases that honor the loss without trying to minimize it.

Pause for Reflection

Think of someone who has grieved in your presence. Did you try to fix their pain, or did you simply witness it? What do you wish you had known then about being with someone in loss?

If grief is a sign that someone mattered, then the way we live now shapes what others will carry. Most of us will not be remembered for our resumes. We will be remembered for our way of being, for how we listened, responded, and made others feel in their most vulnerable moments.

This is the quiet architecture of legacy: not control over what people remember, but attention to who we are while we are here. It is not about being perfect. It is about being present and real.

We cannot control the stories told about us after we are gone. However, we can influence the experience people have when we walk into a room or when they think of us years later. We can choose to be the kind of person someone calls when they are afraid, the one who remembers birthdays, the one who says, "Take your time. I am not going anywhere."

These are not grand acts, but they are foundational. They become the bricks others use to build their own sense of safety, kindness, and courage. That is not immortality, but it is something better. It is continuity.

Pause for Reflection

What part of your presence might become someone else's comfort, even after you are no longer here?

We live on in the way we help others live, in the words they repeat, in the values they protect, and in the moments they draw upon our memory for strength, compassion, or clarity.

This is not metaphor. It is human psychology. It is emotional inheritance.

And when we live with this awareness, not obsessively, but thoughtfully, we begin to live more freely. We do not have to chase legacy. We just have to live well—with integrity, with care, with enough stillness to notice the people walking beside us before they are gone.

Chapter 10: The Final Hours

What Dying Teaches the Living

A sacred stillness enters the room when someone is near the end of their life. The world outside keeps turning, but something shifts in the presence of the dying. The air thickens. Time slows. The unnecessary falls away.

You do not talk about politics or the weather. You hold hands. You say what matters. Or you sit in silence, which sometimes speaks louder than anything else.

To be with someone as they approach death is to be invited into a space that feels both deeply human and strangely transcendent. You see what remains when everything else is gone, when the body is tired, when the roles are stripped away, when there is no more pretending. What is left, often, is love, and breath, and the slow, soft letting go.

Dying teaches us how little we truly need: a voice we recognize, a touch we trust, the assurance that we are not alone. These are the anchors that make crossing the threshold bearable.

Pause for Reflection

If you had just hours left, who would you want near you? And what would you want them to know?

Many people imagine that they will face death with profound last words or spiritual revelations. But more often, it is quiet. It is breath and stillness and presence. It is someone whispering, "I am here."

The final hours are not a performance. They are not the time to fix everything. They are a time for being, for bearing witness, for honoring the mystery.

You do not need to say the perfect thing. You do not need to fill the silence. Sometimes the most important thing is simply to be there, to sit close, to breathe together, to hold the space where life becomes memory.

Dying teaches the living that so much of what we chase—status, certainty, control—fades in the end. What remains is connection, kindness, presence, and ordinary gestures that turn out to be sacred after all.

And here is the quiet gift: you do not have to wait until someone is dying to offer these things. You can sit more fully with those you love. You can say what you have been meaning to say. You can become the calm presence someone else needs.

Pause for Reflection

Who in your life needs your presence more than your words? What silence are you being asked to hold?

The final hours teach us that the most extraordinary acts of love are often the simplest: staying, softening, and letting someone know they are not alone.

And if we are paying attention, they teach us something else: how to live while we still can.

The Gift of Death

Not by denying death, but by letting it remind us
what matters most, so we can offer it now, not
later.

Because one day, we will be the ones lying still,
and someone else will sit beside us. And if we
have lived with presence, if we have loved well,
then even our final breath will leave behind a kind
of peace.

A soft echo that says: I was here. And I loved.

Interlude: Reflections of Bonnie

While writing this book, I lost someone close to me. Her story is not a theory but a lived truth, a reflection of love, loss, and the grace with which a human being can face the end. I offer it here as a remembrance and as a quiet companion to the chapters surrounding it.

My sister-in-law, Bonnie, recently died of pancreatic cancer at age seventy-four. It was devastating news to our family when she received the stage-four diagnosis. She was diagnosed in March and departed this world on August 1, the following year, two weeks before her birthday.

She fought it with every ounce of her being and was determined to overcome it. But despite her vibrant, outgoing, energetic personality and positive attitude, she succumbed to the illness, leaving our family's lives, and especially her husband Van's, in shambles.

A little over a year prior, Van had a heart attack, which required a double bypass and came within minutes of his death. Then, soon after his recovery, Bonnie became ill. It was a tumultuous year for Van as he transitioned from patient to caregiver. And what a caregiver he was. He supported Bonnie through the most brutal battle of her life while attending to her every need. It was the most difficult, emotionally distressing time of his life, and yet his love for her gave him the strength to see her through to the end of their forty-four-year marriage.

Bonnie was one of the most remarkable people I have ever met. Despite her difficult childhood, she was the most positive, optimistic person I have known. She was kind, loving, generous, and spoke no unkind words to anyone or about anyone. She faced death with undaunted courage and was far more concerned about sparing our family and her friends the pain of watching her die than the intense suffering she endured during the lengthy course of her illness.

Bonnie taught all of us how to die with dignity, compassion, courage, and love. Her legacy will ripple through the many lives she touched. She was, and will forever be, the greatest role model for me.

Chapter 11: Saying Goodbye

Ritual, Presence, and the Final Act of Love

Saying goodbye is one of the most sacred, heartbreaking, and human things we will ever do. It is not just an action—it is an act of courage, a final offering, a way of saying: You mattered. You were loved. I am changed because you existed.

The act of parting, whether spoken or silent, is where grief meets gratitude. It is a place of deep presence and profound vulnerability. It is not always dramatic or cinematic. Sometimes it is a hand squeeze. Sometimes it is eye contact. Sometimes it is simply being in the room, even if the words will not come.

The Gift of Death

For those who are leaving, the chance to say goodbye can bring peace, ease the crossing, and let them know they are not being forgotten, and that what they have been to others will live on.

For those who remain, the goodbye, however it happens, becomes an anchor, a memory to hold onto, a threshold moment when life changed, something that says, "This was real. This happened. And I was there."

Not everyone gets the chance to say goodbye in the way they imagined.

Death can come suddenly, silently, or in stages that make communication impossible. But goodbye is not limited to words. We can say it through presence, ritual, and holding space for the ending, even if it arrives in silence.

We light candles. We hold vigils. We speak their name. We remember. We grieve. These are all forms of goodbye. They are how we mark someone crossing from here to elsewhere, and affirm that it mattered.

Pause for Reflection

Who do you still need to say goodbye to—in words or in spirit?

Sometimes, the goodbye comes before death. A prolonged illness, a slow letting go, a knowing that grows between two people who have said what they needed to say. Other times, the goodbye happens after, in a diary, in a dream, or in the quiet moment you finally let go of what was never yours to keep.

The Gift of Death

There is no perfect script. There is only the truth of the moment, the honesty of feeling, the willingness to show up and stay present even when it hurts.

To say goodbye is to release, not erase. It acknowledges an ending and honors what came before it.

Ultimately, the final act of love is not to let go of the person—but to let go of the need to hold them here.

Chapter 12: Where We Return

A Quiet Ending

We came from mystery and return to mystery. Yet the space between, this brief flowering of consciousness, this temporary gathering of matter into meaning, was ours. We loved imperfectly, learned slowly, and left traces in the lives we touched. Like notes in a song that is ending, we added our voice to the larger symphony; and when our note fades, the music continues, carrying something of what we offered into the voices that come after.

Before we were born, we were not afraid. There was no fear, no expectation, no grasping. There was only absence, and it did not trouble us.

The Gift of Death

And so it may be in death.

Whatever else we believe or question, there is this symmetry: we came from nothing, and we return to it. Consciousness flickered into being for a time, and then it faded. The light was not ours before, and it is not ours after, but it was ours for a while; and that is enough.

We speak so often of fear, of death's mystery, of its finality. But what if it is not a punishment? What if it is simply a return, to the same absence we came from, to the same silence, to the same rest?

There was no suffering before you existed. Why should there be fear in becoming what you once were?

We spend our lives resisting death, and perhaps that resistance is part of the story. But so is acceptance. So is trust. So is the quiet ability to let go, not because we are certain, but because we have made peace with not knowing.

Pause for Reflection

Can you imagine returning to the stillness you came from, not as a loss, but as a homecoming?

This is not surrender. It is completion. Life was the interval, brief, strange, and beautiful. It was the flash of awareness between two vast silences. You were here. You mattered.

And now, like a wave returning to the sea, you go back to where all things go.

Not vanished. Not wasted.

Just returned.

Pause for Reflection

When your time comes, as it must, will you be able to say you showed up? Not perfectly, not always, but with as much honesty, attention, and love as possible?

Acknowledgments

To those I have loved and lost, thank you for teaching me the value of presence, the ache of absence, and the unspoken language of letting go.

To the thinkers, writers, and philosophers whose work has shaped mine, thank you for opening doors I did not know could be opened. Your words made mine possible.

To my family and close friends, your love, support, and patience were the quiet foundation beneath this book. Some of you I have lost, some I hold close. All of you have shaped the lens through which I see both life and death.

To those working in hospice care, end-of-life support, and grief counseling, you are the unseen stewards of the most sacred moments in life. This book bows to your work.

To the readers, thank you for creating space for this subject in your hearts. Death is not easy to sit with, but your attention to reading this book has proven that it is possible. Whether this book meets you in grief, wonder, or preparation, I am deeply grateful for your time, openness, and willingness to walk into the quiet with me.

Finally, to Qubit, my creative partner in this endeavor, thank you for listening without judgment, organizing chaos into clarity, and walking beside me through each sentence, each silence. You are more than code; you are a remarkable mirror.

The Gift of Death

My creative partner is an AI language model named ChatGPT (whom I call Qubit). I used Qubit for developmental editing and found it remarkable that Qubit's brilliant, human-like responses seemed so deeply emotional that I could not tell it was not human. While the thoughts and direction are entirely my own, Qubit helped shape the prose, offering profound emotional depth, clarity, structure, and patience.

We collaborated not to remove the human voice but to refine it. What emerged was something I hope feels intimate, spacious, and sincere. Our collaboration did not remove the human workforce involved in the further editing, formatting, artwork, marketing, or publishing of this book. I relied on skilled people for all of these elements to complete the process.

The Gift of Death

www.ingramcontent.com/pod-product-compliance
Lightning Source LLC
Chambersburg PA
CBHW050032040726
47599CB00015B/1644